CW01271967

BIOGRAPHY AND NOVENA TO ST. VALENTINE

Copyright notice

Foreward

The novena dedicated to St. Valentine is a nine-day prayer dedicated to seeking St. Valentine's intercession

A way, you can start by expressing your intentions, thoughts and prayers about things related to love, relationships, or other specific areas of your life.

Maybe you think about different aspects of love every day and seek guidance from St. Valentine.

Table of contents

PART ONE

Early life of St.Valentine

St.Valentine's exact date of birth is unknown as there are few historical records from the 3rd century onwards. Valentine's Day, celebrated on February 14th, is associated with his honor, but his exact birthda remains unknown.Valentine is believed to be his third century Roman saint associated with love and romance. Details of his life are unknown, but he is said to have often officiated at soldiers' weddings, defying Emperor Claudius II's ban on marriage. Legend has it that he sent his first "Valentine" to prison, a note signed "From your Valentine." A security guard's daughter. Over time, it has become a symbol of love and is celebrated every year on Valentine's Day.San Valentino (Saint Valentine) was a 3rd century Roman priest and martyr during the reign of Claudius II, also known as Claudius of the Goths. He was arrested for helping Christians persecuted by Claudius in Rome and for officiating the wedding of a young Christian couple in love Even while imprisoned and threatened, St. Valentine did not hesitate to answer the emperor's questions about his faith.The Emperor attempts to convert Saint Valentine, but to no avail. However, no matter what he was asked, Valentine refused to renounce his faith, so Claudius sent him to prison.The jailer where Valentine was imprisoned listened to his sermons day in and day out.According to legend, the patron Asterius had a blind daughter. He asked Valentin to hear her confession, and he complied.Then Valentine put his hands on the girl's eyes and sang: "Lord Jesus Christ, shine on your handmaiden, for you are God and the true light." Immediately the girl regained her sight.Thanks to this miracle, the prison guard and many of his family members converted to Christianity and were baptized.Emperor Claudius heard about the conversions and condemned them all. On the eve of his execution, Valentine wrote a note to the girl and signed it "From your Valentine," after which he was clubbed, stoned, and finally beheaded on February 14,

circa 269 AD. It was done. He was buried in Via Flaminana, and a chapel was later built over his body.On the same day, another Bishop of Terni, Valentinus, was imprisoned and beheaded by Placidus, Governor of Terni, about 60 miles outside Rome. Many people mysteriously believe that these two men are the same priest - the same Valentine who was previously taken to Rome for execution and buried in Via Flaminana.

PART TWO

9 Days Novena prayers to St.Valentine

Day 1 Prayer

In the name of the father, and of the son, and of the holy spirit Amen.

O, Saint Valentine, glorious intercessor and protector, look with mercy on our needs, hear our supplications, hear our prayers.By your intercession, alleviate the misery we are suffering, and obtain for us the blessings of God to which we are deemed worthy to partake. You will forever praise the Almighty.

By the merits of our Lord Jesus

Christ.

Therefore, holy martyr, pray for the faithful who persistently celebrate your memory.

On the Day of Judgment, all your glorious deeds will be revealed to us.

oh!

Please intercede for us.

Then we may become your companions at the right hand of the great Judge and be united to you forever in heaven.

Let us pray: Grant, Almighty God, as we celebrate the Feast of Your Martyr St.

Valentine, may by His intercession be delivered from all the evil that threatens us.

Through Christ our Lord.

Amen

Saint Valentine, advocate and protector, pray for us.

Saint Valentine, patron saint of love and relationships, I ask for your intercession. Help me to grow love in my heart and share it with others.

Our Father

Hail Mary

Glory be

Day 2 Prayer

In the name of the father, and of the son, and of the holy spirit. Amen

O, Glorious Intercessor and Protector, Saint Valentine, look with compassion on our needs, hear our requests, hear our prayers.

By your intercession, alleviate the misery we suffer and obtain for us the blessings of God that we deserve.

Join us in praising the Almighty forever.

By the merits of our Lord Jesus Christ.

Therefore, holy martyr, pray for the faithful who persistently celebrate your memory.

On the Day of Judgment, all your glorious deeds will be revealed to us.

oh!

Please intercede for us.

Then we may become your companions at the right hand of the great Judge and be united to you forever in heaven.

Let us pray: Grant, Almighty God, as we celebrate the Feast of Your Martyr St.

Valentine, may by His intercession be delivered from all the evil that threatens us.

Through Christ our Lord.

Amen.

Saint Valentine, advocate and protector, pray for us.

St. Valentine,Please guide me to understand the true meaning of love.

 May my relationships be based on compassion, patience, and kindness.

Our Father

Hail Mary

Glory be.

Day 3 Prayer

In the name of the father, and of the son, and of the holy spirit. Amen

O, Glorious Intercessor and Guardian, St.

Valentine, look with compassion on our needs, hear our supplications, hear our prayers.

By your intercession, alleviate the misery we suffer and obtain for us the blessing of God, that we may be recognized as worthy.

I will praise you forever, Almighty.

By the merits of our Lord Jesus Christ.

Therefore, holy martyr, pray for the faithful who persistently celebrate your memory.

On the Day of Judgment, all your glorious deeds will be revealed to us.

oh!

Please intercede for us.

Then we may become your companions at the right hand of the great Judge and be united to you forever in heaven.

Let us pray: Grant, Almighty God, as we celebrate the Feast of Your Martyr St.

Valentine, may by His intercession be delivered from all the evil that threatens us.

Through Christ our Lord.

Amen.

St.Valentine advocate, and protector, pray for us

St. Valentine, Bless my friendships and family Bless my friendships and family ties.

May they be always be reminded of ur
blessings and love

Our Father

Hail Mary

Glory be

Day 4 Prayer

In the name of the son, and of the son, and of the holy spirit. Amen

O, Glorious Intercessor and Guardian, St.

Valentine, look with compassion on our needs, hear our supplications, hear our prayers.

By your intercession, alleviate the misery we suffer and obtain for us the blessing of God, that we may be recognized as worthy.

I will praise you forever, Almighty.

By the merits of our Lord Jesus Christ.

Therefore, holy martyr, pray for the faithful who persistently celebrate your memory.

On the Day of Judgment, all your

glorious deeds will be revealed to us.

oh!

Please intercede for us.

Then we may become your companions at the right hand of the great Judge and be united to you forever in heaven.

Let us pray: Grant, Almighty God, as we celebrate the Feast of Your Martyr St.

Valentine, may by His intercession be delivered from all the evil that threatens us.

Through Christ our Lord.

Amen.

St. Valentine advocate, and protector, pray for us
St. Valentine,Intercession for those seeking love.

May they find comfort and experience the beauty of a great loving relationship .

Our Father

Hail Mary

Glory be

Day 5 Prayer

In the name of the father, and of the son, and of the holy spirit. Amen

O glorious advocate and protector, Saint Valentine, look with pity upon our wants, hear our requests, attend to our prayers, relieve by your intercession the miseries under which we labor, and obtain for us the Divine blessing, that we may be found worthy to join thee in praising the Almighty for all eternity; through the merits of Our Lord Jesus Christ.

Pray, then, O holy Martyr, for the faithful, who are so persevering in celebrating thy memory. The day of Judgment will reveal to us all thy glorious merits. Oh! intercede

for us, that we may then be made thy companions at the right hand of the Great Judge, and be united with thee eternally in heaven.

Let us pray: Grant, we beseech thee, O Almighty God, that we who solemnize the festival of blessed Valentine, Thy Martyr, may, by his intercession, be delivered from all the evils that threaten us. Through Christ our Lord. Amen.

Saint Valentine, advocate and protector, pray for us.

St. Valentine, Encourage yourself to truly love yourself and others.Please grant me the wisdom to understand the uniqueness of each person in my life.

Our Father

Hail Mary

Glory be

Day 6 Prayer

In the name of the father, and of the son, and of the holy spirit. Amen

O, Glorious Intercessor and Guardian, St.

Valentine, look with compassion on our Daily needs, hear our supplications, hear our prayers.

By your intercession, alleviate the misery we suffer and obtain for us the blessing of God, that we may be recognized as worthy.

I will praise you forever, Almighty.

By the merits of our Lord Jesus Christ.

Therefore, holy martyr, pray for the faithful who persistently celebrate your memory.

On the Day of Judgment, all your glorious deeds will be revealed to us.

oh!

Please intercede for us.

Then we may become your companions at the right hand of the great Judge and be united to you forever in heaven.

Let us pray: Grant, Almighty God, as we celebrate the Feast of Your Martyr St.

Valentine, may by His intercession be delivered from all the evil that threatens us.

Through Christ our Lord.

Amen.

St.Valentine advocate, and protector, pray for us

St. Valentine, Please help me heal all the wounds in my relationships.

May forgiveness and understanding prevail in moments of conflict.

Our Father

Hail Mary

Glory be

Day 7 Prayer

In the name of the father, and of the son, and of the holy spirit. Amen

O glorious advocate and protector, Saint Valentine, look with pity upon our wants, hear our requests, attend to our prayers, relieve by your intercession the miseries under which we labor, and obtain for us the Divine blessing, that we may be found worthy to join thee in praising the Almighty for all eternity; through the merits of Our Lord Jesus Christ.

Pray, then, O holy Martyr, for the faithful, who are so persevering in celebrating thy memory. The day of Judgment will reveal to us all thy glorious merits. Oh! intercede

for us, that we may then be made thy companions at the right hand of the Great Judge, and be united with thee eternally in heaven.

Let us pray: Grant, we beseech thee, O Almighty God, that we who solemnize the festival of blessed Valentine, Thy Martyr, may, by his intercession, be delivered from all the evils that threaten us. Through Christ our Lord. Amen.

St. Valentine advocate, and protector, pray for us

St. Valentine, Blessings to all who are married or considering marriage.

Strengthen your commitment and deepen your love for each other.

Our Father

Hail Mary

Glory be

Day 8 Prayer

In the name of the father, and of the son, and of the holy spirit. Amen

O glorious advocate and protector, Saint Valentine, look with pity upon our wants, hear our requests, attend to our prayers, relieve by your intercession the miseries under which we labor, and obtain for us the Divine blessing, that we may be found worthy to join thee in praising the Almighty for all eternity; through the merits of Our Lord Jesus Christ.

Pray, then, O holy Martyr, for the faithful, who are so persevering in celebrating thy memory. The day of Judgment will reveal to us all thy glorious merits. Oh! intercede

for us, that we may then be made thy companions at the right hand of the Great Judge, and be united with thee eternally in heaven.

Let us pray: Grant, we beseech thee, O Almighty God, that we who solemnize the festival of blessed Valentine, Thy Martyr, may, by his intercession, be delivered from all the evils that threaten us. Through Christ our Lord. Amen.

Saint Valentine, advocate and protector, pray for us.
St. Valentine, protect all the lonely and heartbroken.

It brings comfort to their souls and leads them to love and connection.

Our Father

Hail Mary

Glory be

Day 9 Prayer

In the name of the father, and of the son, and of the holy spirit. Amen

O, Glorious Intercessor and Protector, Saint Valentine, look with compassion on our needs, hear our requests, hear our prayers.

By your intercession, alleviate the misery we suffer and obtain for us the blessings of God that we deserve.

Join us in praising the Almighty forever.

By the merits of our Lord Jesus Christ.

Therefore, holy martyr, pray for

the faithful who persistently celebrate your memory.

On the Day of Judgment, all your glorious deeds will be revealed to us.

Please intercede for us.

Then we may become your companions at the right hand of the great Judge and be united to you forever in heaven.

Let us pray: Grant, Almighty God, as we celebrate the Feast of Your Martyr St.

Valentine, may by His intercession be delivered from all the evil that threatens us.

Through Christ our Lord.

Amen.

Saint Valentine, advocate and protector, pray for us.

St. Valentine, As I conclude this novena, I would like to express my gratitude for your intercession.

May love in all its forms continue to flourish in my life.

Our Father

Hail Mary

Glory be

Printed in Great Britain
by Amazon

57991292R00020